Christmas Cookbook

Homemade Recipes for Happy Holidays

Table of Contents

Biscuit Recipes

Ginger cookie sandwiches with lemon mascarpone

PREP: 30 mins

COOK: 14 mins

MAKES 12-15

ingredients

- ✓ 2 Tbsps. golden caster sugar
- ✓ 4 Tbsps. unsalted butter, melted

- ✓ 1 Tbsp. black treacle
- ✓ 4 Tbsps. light brown soft sugar
- ✓ 1 large egg
- ✓ ½ tsp. vanilla extract
- ✓ 1 cup and 2 Tbsps. gluten-free flour blend
- ✓ ¼ tsp. bicarbonate of soda
- ✓ ½ tsp. ground black pepper
- ✓ 1 tsp. ground ginger
- ✓ ¼ tsp. ground cloves
- ✓ ¼ tsp. ground nutmeg
- ✓ ¼ tsp. ground cardamom
- ✓ 2-3 Tbsps. demerara sugar, to coat

For the filling

- ✓ 3 oz lemon curd
- ✓ 6 oz mascarpone

method

The cookies

- ✓ Put the sugars, butter, vanilla, treacle, and egg in a large bowl and mix with an electric whisk until combined and smooth. In the other bowl mix the remaining ingredients except for the demerara. Add the dry ingredients to the egg mixture and stir until a very sticky dough is formed. Wrap with cling film and cool for at least 4 hours.

- ✓ Heat oven to 320F (160C) gas 4 / 360F (180C) fan and line two baking sheets with baking paper. Make the cookie dough into balls, about a Tbsp. in size and roll in the demerara sugar. Put on the trays, leaving about 1 inch space between cookies.
- ✓ Bake for about 14 minutes or until just lightly browned around the sides, swapping the trays over halfway through cooking. Allow cooling on the trays for 10 minutes before replacing to a wire rack to cool thoroughly.

The filling

- ✓ Stir together the lemon curd and mascarpone in a bowl until creamy and smooth. Place in a piping bag with a plain round tip. Pipe a layer of the cream onto the bottom of the cookies and join together with the other cookie. You can keep cookies for 3-4 days in an airtight container in the fridge – the texture will become soft and cakey (this is normal).

Orange & ginger stained glass biscuits

PREP: 15 mins

COOK: 20 mins

MAKES 14

ingredients

- ✓ sunflower oil, for greasing
- ✓ 1 cup and 2 Tbsps. plain flour, plus extra
- ✓ 1 tsp. ground ginger
- ✓ zest 1 orange
- ✓ 4–5 Tbsps. butter, cold, cut into chunks
- ✓ 2 Tbsps. golden caster sugar
- ✓ 1 Tbsp. milk
- ✓ icing sugar, to dust
- ✓ 12 fruit-flavored boiled sweets
- ✓ 4 feets (120cm) thin ribbon, to decorate

method

- ✓ Heat oven to 320F (160C) gas 4 / 356C (180C) fan. Grease 2 large non-stick baking trays with oil. Mix the butter, flour, ginger, 1/2 tsp. salt, and zest to fine crumbs in a food processor. Add the milk and sugar, then turn out and knead briefly on a lightly floured surface until smooth. Cover with cling film, then cool for about 30 minutes.
- ✓ Flour the work surface again, then roll out the dough to the thickness of a 0.2in (5mm). Take 3in (7cm) cutters and cut out shapes, then take 1.5in (4cm) cutters and cut out the middles. Re-roll remaining pieces. Make a hole in the top of each cookie, then carefully transfer to the baking sheets.
- ✓ Press the sweets under their covers with a rolling pin, then put the slices into the centers of the biscuits – the sweets should be level with the top of the dough. Bake for 15-20 minutes or until the middles have melted and the biscuits are golden brown.
- ✓ Leave to harden, then place to a rack to cool. Thread with ribbon, then dust with icing sugar.

Will keep for a month, but best eaten within 3 days.

Snowy owl Christmas tree biscuits

PREP: 1 hr

COOK: 8 - 14 mins

MAKES about 6 large, 5 medium or 8 small owls

ingredients

For the biscuits

- ✓ 5 Tbsps. slightly salted butter softened
- ✓ 5 Tbsps. caster sugar
- ✓ 1 egg, lightly beaten
- ✓ 1 tsp vanilla extract
- ✓ 1 ½ cups plain flour

For the decoration

- ✓ 3.5 oz. (100g) packet of whole blanched almond

- ✓ 4.5 oz. (130g) packet of giant white chocolate button
- ✓ 0.7 oz. (20g) packet standard-sized white chocolate button
- ✓ 3.5 oz. (100g) packet of flaked almond, toasted
- ✓ 1.7 oz.(50g) dark chocolate chip
- ✓ icing sugar, for dusting
- ✓ fine string, for hanging the biscuits
- ✓ gold edible glitter (optional)

method

- ✓ Heat the oven to 340F (170C) gas 5 / 380F (190C) fan. Beat together the butter and sugar, then slowly beat in the egg and vanilla extract. Sift and mix in the flour and stir into a soft dough. Transfer to a lightly floured area and knead gently. Wrap or cover the dough in cling film and cool for at least 2 hours.
- ✓ Roll the dough out on a lightly floured area to about 0.2in (5mm) thick. Cut into oval shapes.
- ✓ Replace the biscuits to a baking sheet lined with baking parchment. Put differently sized cookies on different trays. Put the whole almonds into

the dough to create the owls' beaks and eyebrows. If creating decorations for the tree, make a hole near the top of the biscuits using the straw. Bake for 8 - 14 minutes, depending on the size of the cookies until the edges turn lightly golden. Then leave the biscuits on the baking sheet to chill.

✓ Make the owls' eyes white chocolate buttons. Melt the remainder in the microwave or a bowl over almost boiling water.

✓ Stick on the white chocolate buttons, then the dark chocolate pieces on top to make the eyes. You can layer the almonds with other white chocolate.

✓ Thread pretty string or fine ribbon into Christmas decorations so you can hang them. Dust with icing sugar and gold edible glitter if using.

Orange & cardamom tree biscuits

PREP: 30 - 40 mins

COOK: 12 - 15 mins

MAKES 25

ingredients

- ✓ 1 ½ cups plain flour
- ✓ 3 Tbsps. rice flour
- ✓ 5 Tbsps. butter
- ✓ 6 cardamom pods
- ✓ 1 egg yolk
- ✓ grated zest 1 orange
- ✓ 4 Tbsps. icing sugar, plus extra to decorate

You'll also need

- ✓ cocktail sticks

13

- ✓ pastry cutters
- ✓ Christmas rubber stamps and thin ribbon or string

method

- ✓ Split the cardamom pods and place the seeds into a mortar, then chop to a powder with the pestle. Add the cardamom powder, flour, rice flour into a food processor. Cut the butter into small pieces. Add the orange zest and butter to the food processor. Pulse to a fine breadcrumb texture. Add the icing sugar and mix quickly, then add 1-2 tsps. cold water and the egg yolk and pulse to a firm dough. Wrap in cling film and cool for 15 mins.
- ✓ Heat oven to 320F (160C) gas 4 / 360F (180C) fan. Line 2 baking trays with baking parchment. Roll out half the dough and stamp out 3in (7cm) squares or rounds and transfer to the baking trays. Make a hole with a stick in each biscuit for hanging to the tree. Press a festive rubber stamp into the surface of each biscuit. Cool for 30 minutes.
- ✓ Bake for 8-10 minutes until crisp and just golden. Chill on the wire rack.
- ✓ Dust each biscuit liberally with icing sugar, then brush off the excess from the surface, leaving a white imprint on each biscuit. Tie up with pretty ribbon or string and hang from your tree.

Gingerbread people

PREP: 45 mins

SCOOK: 12 - 15 mins

SERVES 15 - 20

ingredients

- ✓ 1 cup dark muscovado sugar
- ✓ 3 oz. (85g) golden syrup
- ✓ 5 Tbsps. butter
- ✓ 2 cups plain flour, plus extra for dusting
- ✓ 1 tsp. bicarbonate of soda
- ✓ 1 tsp. ground ginger

- ✓ 1 tsp. ground cinnamon
- ✓ 1 egg, beaten

To decorate

- ✓ chocolate buttons or small sweets (optional)
- ✓ ready-made writing icing

method

- ✓ Melt the golden syrup, butter, and sugar, in a saucepan, and bubble for 1-2 minutes. Let it cool for about 10 minutes.
- ✓ Tip the bicarbonate of soda, spices, and flour, in a large bowl. Add the egg and the warm syrup mixture, mix everything, then gently knead in the bowl until streak-free and smooth. The dough will firm up once chilled. Cover with cling film and cool for at least 30 minutes.
- ✓ Transfer the dough from the fridge, leave at room temperature until softened. Heat an oven to 360F (180C) gas 6 / 390F (200C) fan and line two cookie sheets with baking parchment.
- ✓ Roll out the dough to the thickness of about 0.1in (3mm), then cut out gingerbread people. Re-roll the extra dough and keep cutting until it's all used up.
- ✓ Remove the biscuits to the cookie sheets and bake for 10-12 mins, swapping the trays over halfway while

cooking. Let to cool on the trays for 5 minutes, then move to a wire rack to cool thoroughly. Use the icing to decorate the cookies as you wish, and stick to sweets for buttons. Leave to dry for 1-2 hours. You can keep cookies for up to three days in an airtight container.

Cinnamon stars

PREP: 30 mins

COOK: 15 mins

MAKES ABOUT 30

ingredients

- ✓ 1 tsp. lemon juice
- ✓ 1 lemon's zest
- ✓ 2 tsps. ground cinnamon
- ✓ 1 cup icing sugar, plus extra for dusting
- ✓ 2 large egg whites
- ✓ 1 tsp. ground ginger
- ✓ 8 oz. (225g) ground almond

method

- ✓ Heat oven to 260F (130C) gas 2 / 300F (150C) fan and line a baking tray with baking parchment. Beat the egg whites in a large pot. Use an electric mixer to whisk until creamy. Add the lemon juice and whisk until they are soft peaks.

✓ Carefully stir in the icing sugar and whisk until the mixture is thick. Transfer about a quarter of the meringue mixture and set aside to use for the topping. Put the lemon zest almonds, cinnamon, ginger and in the bowl with the meringue and stir to form a slightly sticky, stiff dough.

✓ To form the stars, place the dough on a piece of baking parchment lightly powdered with icing sugar and powder the top of the dough with sugar, too. Put another piece of parchment on top of the dough and roll out to about 0.2in (5mm) thick. Peel off the top sheet of parchment and use a 2in (5cm) star-shaped cutter to cut out as many cookies as possible. Place them on your prepared baking tray.

✓ Using the reserved meringue mixture, spread a small amount onto the top of each cookie, covering the entire top – you may need to add a few drops of water to make the meringue a little easier to spread. Put the tray in the oven and bake for 12-15 mins until meringue is set but not browned. Allow cooling completely before storing in a sealed container for up to 2 weeks

Edible name place biscuits.

TIME: 30 mins

MAKES 4

ingredients

- ✓ 4 giant cookies
- ✓ ½ tsp. peppermint extract
- ✓ 2 cups icing sugar
- ✓ sprinkles and sweets, to decorate

method

- ✓ Mix peppermint extract with icing sugar and enough
  water to make a thick icing. Spread the icing over

cookies and create a border around the edges using sweets and sprinkles. Leave for 10 mins for the icing to set.

✓ Then, using an icing pen, write a guest's name in the center of each biscuit. When the icing is dry, wrap in cellophane and tie up with a nice ribbon.

Double chocolate & orange biscotti

PREP: 15 mins

COOK: 1 hr

MAKES 8-10

ingredients

- ✓ 4 oz. self-raising flour
- ✓ 1 Tbsp. cocoa powder
- ✓ 2 oz. ground almonds
- ✓ 3 Tbsps. golden caster sugar
- ✓ 2 oz. dark chocolate chips
- ✓ 1.4 oz. candied peel
- ✓ 1 large orange, zested
- ✓ ¼ whole nutmeg, grated

- ✓ 1 tsp. vanilla extract
- ✓ 1 large egg
- ✓ 1 egg yolk, beaten

method

- ✓ Warm up the oven to 320F (160C) gas 4 / 360F (180C) fan. Put the cocoa, ground almonds, chocolate chips, flour, sugar, candied peel, orange zest and a pinch of salt in a large bowl, and stir well. Make a well in the center, then add the vanilla essence and egg. Bring the mix together by your hands, stirring it firmly.
- ✓ Form the biscotti dough into a log approximately 6in x 2in x 1in (15cm x 5cm x 2.5cm) deep. Remove to a cookie sheet lined with baking parchment, then bake for 30 minutes. The log will split and crack a little on the top.
- ✓ Transfer from the oven and cool for at least 10 minutes. Cut the log into slices 0.5in (12mm) thick, using a sharp serrated knife
- ✓ Put the biscotti again on the cookie sheet and reduce oven to 260F (130C) gas 2 / 300F (150C) fan. Bake for 30 minutes or until the biscotti are completely hard to touch. Cool completely, then wrap in baking parchment or store in an airtight container.

Vegan gingerbread people

PREP: 30 mins

COOK: 10 - 12 mins

MAKES AROUND 20

ingredients

- ✓ 2 ½ cups plain flour, plus extra for dusting
- ✓ 1 Tbsp. chia seeds
- ✓ 2 Tbsps. ground ginger
- ✓ 1 cup dark muscovado sugar
- ✓ 1 cup coconut oil
- ✓ 1 tsp. ground cinnamon
- ✓ ½ cup aquafaba (water from a can of chickpeas)
- ✓ 2 Tbsps. maple syrup
- ✓ ½ tsp. lemon juice

✓ 2 cups icing sugar

method

✓ Mix the chia seeds with 3 Tbsps. water in a small bowl. Leave to soak for 5-10 minutes until gloopy. Meantime, put the flour into a large mixing bowl and add the coconut oil until it's almost disappeared into the flour. Add the spices.
✓ In another bowl mix 2 Tbsps. water, the chia mixture, sugar, maple syrup until smooth and pour over the flour. Stir until well combined then and make a soft dough. Wrap in cling film.
✓ Heat oven to 320F (160C) gas 6 / 360F (180C) fan. Roll out the dough on a gently floured area then cut into gingerbread people and bake for 10-12 minutes on baking trays lined with baking paper until just starting to darken at the edges. Let them chill for a couple of minutes on the sheet then transfer to a wire rack to chill completely.
✓ While the gingerbread chills whip the aquafaba in a bowl using electric mixers until really foamy. Add 3/4 of the icing sugar and mix until smooth and thick, then stir in the lemon juice and the rest of the icing sugar. Mix again until the mixture forms stiff peaks. Replace to a piping bag until ready to use. Snip a little off the end of the piping bag and use to create designs and faces on your gingerbread.

Melting snowman biscuits

TIME: 30 mins

MAKES 6

ingredients

- ✓ 1 cup fondant icing sugar
- ✓ 6 white marshmallows
- ✓ 6 large cookies
- ✓ 6 pretzel sticks
- ✓ tube black writing icing
- ✓ 24 mini chocolate beans

method

- ✓ Place the icing sugar in a bowl. Then add cold water one tsp. at a time until the dough is runny but thick enough to coat a spoon.
- ✓ Snip the marshmallows in half with wetted scissors.
- ✓ Add a little icing to each cookie and a half of marshmallow. Through a little icing, stick the other half of marshmallow on top at an angle. Drizzle more glaze onto the cookie to make melting snow.
- ✓ Cut the pretzel sticks in half and add on the cookie for arms. Stick three chocolate beans on each cookie to represent buttons. Stick orange chocolate beans on for the noses.
- ✓ Using the writing icing, pipe small blobs for the eyes and mouth. Leave to set.

Fruity biscotti

PREP: 15 mins

COOK: 1 hr

MAKES ABOUT 72 biscuits

ingredients

- ✓ 2 ½ cups plain flour, plus extra for rolling
- ✓ 2 tsps. baking powder
- ✓ 2 tsps. mixed spice
- ✓ 1 cup and 2 Tbsps. golden caster sugar
- ✓ 3 eggs, beaten
- ✓ coarsely grated zest 1 orange
- ✓ 3 oz. (85g) raisin
- ✓ 3 oz. (85g) dried cherry
- ✓ 2 oz. (55g) shelled pistachio
- ✓ 2 oz. (55g) blanched almond

method

✓ Heat oven to 320F (160C) gas 4 / 360F (180C) fan. Line 2 baking sheets with baking parchment. Put the baking powder, flour, sugar, and spice in a large bowl, then mix well. Mix in the zest and eggs until the mixture starts forming clumps, then knead the dough with your hands – it may seem dry but keep kneading until no floury spots remain. Add the nuts and fruit, then work them in until evenly dispersed.

✓ Turn the dough out onto a lightly floured surface and divide into 4 equal pieces. With easily floured hands, roll each piece into a log about 30cm long. Place two on each sheet. Bake for 25-30 minutes till the dough has spread and risen and feels firm. It will still look pale. Transfer from the oven put on a wire rack for a few minutes until cold enough, then turn down the oven to 250F (120C) gas 1 / 280F (140C) fan.

✓ Take a bread knife and cut into slices about 1cm thick on the diagonal, then lay the slices on the baking trays. Bake for another 15 minutes, turn over, then bake again for another 15 minutes until dry and golden. Put to a wire rack to cool completely, then store in an airtight tin for up to one month, or pack into boxes or cellophane bags if giving as gifts straightaway.

Rudolph shortbread

PREP: 35 mins

COOK: 25 mins

MAKES 8 big biscuits

ingredients

- ✓ 3 Tbsps. golden caster sugar
- ✓ 5 Tbsps. salted butter, softened
- ✓ 2 tsps. vanilla extract
- ✓ 1.5 cups plain flour, plus extra for dusting
- ✓ 3 oz. (85g) ground rice
- ✓ 3 Tbsps. icing sugar
- ✓ 16 white chocolate buttons or white sweets for the eyes
- ✓ black writing icing tube
- ✓ 8 red Smarties

You will also need

- ✓ 8 brown pipe cleaners
- ✓ cellophane squares or cellophane bags (6 x 10in / 15 x 25 cm)
- ✓ 9in (23cm) round plate, cake tin or cardboard template
- ✓ labels and string or ribbon

method

- ✓ Put the vanilla, sugar, and butter in a big mixing bowl and mix with a wooden spoon until really soft. Add the ground rice and then the flour. If it starts to get dry, you might need to use your hands to squish everything together to make a soft dough.
- ✓ Line a baking tray with a piece of baking parchment. Form the dough into a round ball in the middle of the parchment, then push it down and flatten it using your hands. Take a rolling pin and dust it with some flour, so it doesn't stick to the dough. Roll the dough out to a big circle.
- ✓ Take a 9in round plate, cardboard template or cake tin and place on top of the dough. Use a cutlery knife to cut around the edges to make a nice circle.
- ✓ Mark the giant biscuit with a knife into eight smaller wedge-shaped cookies (but don't cut it). Prick lines from the edge to the center of the dough. Take a fork

and make a line pattern - press all around the top of the circle along the edge (it's going to be hair for your reindeer!)

- ✓ Wrap with cling film and put the tray in the fridge for 30 minutes to get cold. Heat oven to 320F (160C) gas 4 / 360F (180C) fan. Cook the chilled shortbread for 25 minutes until golden. Cool thoroughly on the tray, then use a sharp knife to follow the lines you made and cut into eight wedges.

- ✓ Combine the icing sugar with 1-2 tsps. of water to make an icing. Dunk each Smartie in an icing and stick one on the pointy end of each biscuit to make red noses. Dunk in your chocolate buttons or white sweets and stick them 0.8in (2cm) in from the edge at the other end to make eyes. Use the black writing icing tube to make dots on the white eyes, then let all the icing dry and become hard.

- ✓ Carefully put each biscuit in a cellophane bag or cover in a square of cellophane. Gathered cellophane to enclose the biscuit or twist the middle of a pipe cleaner in a loop around the top of the bag. Then wrap the pipe cleaner, so it looks like the reindeer's antlers. Hang on the tree or add labels and give to your friends and family. Keep your biscuits for up to 3 days in a cool, dry place.

Sugar-dusted vanilla thins

TIME: 20 mins

MAKES 35 biscuits

ingredients

- ✓ 1 quantity vanilla shortbread dough
- ✓ icing sugar, for dusting

method

- ✓ With your hands, make the dough on a lightly floured surface into a sausage shape about 2in (5cm) in diameter and 9in (25cm)long. Wrap the roll and cold for at least 1 hour.

✓ Heat the oven to 320F (160C) gas 4 / 360F (180C) fan and lightly grease two large baking trays. Take a sharp knife and sliced the dough into slices, each ¼in (5mm) thick, then transfer them on the greased baking sheets, spacing the biscuits slightly apart, so they have a bit of room to spread as they cook.

✓ Bake for 20 minutes until the biscuits are just turning pale golden around the edges, then replace to a wire rack to cool. Dust freely with icing sugar. Will keep fresh for up to one week stored in an airtight tin.

Sparkling vanilla Christmas cookies

PREP: 10 mins

COOK: 12 mins

MAKES 20 biscuits

ingredients

- ✓ 5 oz. (140g) icing sugar sieved
- ✓ 1 tsp. vanilla extract
- ✓ 1 egg yolk
- ✓ 9 oz (250g) butter, cut into small cubes
- ✓ 13 oz (375g) plain flour sieved

<ins>*To decorate*</ins>

- ✓ 7 oz (200g) icing sugar sieved

35

- ✓ edible food coloring, optional
- ✓ approx 2m thin ribbon cut into 10cm lengths
- ✓ edible gold and silver balls

method

- ✓ Put the vanilla extract, butter, icing sugar, and egg yolk into a large bowl, then pulse in a food processor or stir together with a wooden spoon until well mixed. Add the flour and knead to a thick dough. Roll the dough into two flat discs and wrap in cling film. Chill for 20-30 minutes. Heat oven to 340F (170C) gas 5 / 380F(190C) fan and line two baking trays with baking parchment.
- ✓ Roll out the dough on a lightly floured area to about the thickness of 0.1in (2-3mm). Cut out Christmassy shapes and transfer on the baking sheets. Using the cocktail stick make a small hole in the top of each biscuit. Bake for 10-12 minutes until lightly golden.
- ✓ Transfer the biscuits to a wire rack to chill. Meanwhile, stir the icing sugar with a few drops of cold water to make a thick, but still runny icing. Color with edible food colouring, if you like. Spread it over the cooled biscuits, decorate with edible balls and thread with ribbon when dry.

Gingerbread bunting

PREP: 1 hr, 30 mins

COOK: 15 mins

MAKES ABOUT 16 biscuits

ingredients

For the gingerbread

- ✓ 3 oz (85g) golden syrup
- ✓ 6 oz (175g) muscovado sugar, plus a little extra for the reindeer
- ✓ 3.5 oz (100g) butter
- ✓ 12 oz (350g) plain flour, plus extra for dusting
- ✓ 1 tsp bicarbonate of soda
- ✓ 1 tbsp ground ginger

- ✓ 1 tsp ground cinnamon
- ✓ 1 egg, lightly beaten

To decorate

- ✓ brown and black food coloring
- ✓ 21 oz (600g) fondant icing sugar
- ✓ edible white or silver glitter
- ✓ sweets and sprinkles

You'll also need

- ✓ gingerbread lady cutter
- ✓ gingerbread man cutter
- ✓ disposable piping bags
- ✓ small piping nozzle
- ✓ a straw
- ✓ ribbon or string, to tie together
- ✓ cocktail sticks

method

- ✓ Put the butter, syrup, a pinch of salt and sugar into a saucepan. Bubble for 1-2 minutes, mixing. Set apart to cool a little. Put the bicarbonate of soda, spices, and flour in a bowl, add the egg and the warm syrup mixture, and mix to combine (it will be a little soft now, but will firm up once cooled). Coat the bowl with cling film and chill for 30 minutes. Heat oven to 360F (180C) gas 6 / 390F (200C) fan and line two baking sheets with parchment.

✓ Powder your work area with a little flour, then roll out the dough to the thickness of a 0.1in (2-3 mm). Cut out as many ladies and men as you can. Place on the trays then bakes for 10-12 minutes until golden brown and slightly risen. While they are still warm, stick a straw just above where the legs meet on the gingerbread men, and through the top of the gingerbread ladies to make a hole for stringing up. Chill on a wire rack.

Decoration:

✓ Divide the icing sugar evenly among two bowls. Pour enough water, a splash at a time, until you have a very thick icing. Add some drops of brown food coloring to one bowl of icing and mix until evenly colored. Place 2 tbsp of the brown icing into another bowl, then color black using the black food coloring.

✓ Transfer about half the white icing to a piping bag fitted with a narrow nozzle. Pipe the shape of a snowman onto the gingerbread lady, piping a little circle around the hole at the top. Leave to set for 5 minutes. Remove any remaining icing back into the bowl with the white icing and add a little more water, a dribble at a time, until runny but still fairly thick. Remove back to the piping bag. When the snowman edges are dry to the touch, add enough icing to the biscuits to fill the surface. Tease the icing on all corners using a cocktail stick.

- ✓ Use half an silver balls for the buttons and orange jelly bean for the nose. Remove the black and brown icings to piping bags fitted with tiny nozzles (or snip off the corner of a sandwich bag). Pipe on black dots as coal for eyes and a mouth and brown twigs for arms. Sprinkle the base of each snowman with some edible glitter. Leave to dry for at least 2 hours.

Raindeer:

- ✓ Draw a reindeer shape on each gingerbread man biscuit with the brown icing. Turn them upside down first so you can use the gingerbread man's legs as the reindeer's antlers.
- ✓ Fill each reindeer with the brown icing. Be careful not to make the antlers too thick. Tease the icing on all corners with a cocktail stick. Scatter each antler with brown sugar. Stick two white chocolate chips on each biscuit for eyes and a red ball or Smartie for a nose. Use some black icing to draw a pupil in each eye. Leave to dry for at least 2 hours.
- ✓ When the biscuits are fully dry, tie through a piece of string and hang. Eat the biscuits within 2 weeks.

Christmas Dinner Ideas

Bacon roast pork tenderloin

SERVES 2

ingredients

- ✓ 3-4 slices of bacon
- ✓ 1 lb pork tenderloin
- ✓ 1 Tbsp brown sugar (or your favorite sweet)
- ✓ 1 Tbsp any mustard
- ✓ ½ tsp salt
- ✓ 1 tsp herb or spice, ground cinnamon dried thyme or fresh rosemary

✓ lots of freshly cracked black pepper

method

✓ Heat the oven to 500F (260C). Switch on the convection fan if you have it. Line a baking sheet with a baking parchment.

✓ Neatly slice off and remove the 'silverskin' from the tenderloin, leaving any visible fat. In a small bowl mix the mustard, your preferred herb or spice and the brown sugar. With your hands, dip the tenderloin and coat well. Spice it with pepper, then fold under the small end of the tenderloin, so it doesn't overcook. Wrap the bacon all around with a slight overlap trying to have your starts and finishes on the bottom. Secure the bacon by stabbing through with a piece of dry spaghetti noodle and place on the prepared baking sheet. Add some more pepper over and bake to the temperature of 145F (60C), about 20min. Slice, serve and share!

Overnight-baked ham with riesling-mustard glaze

ingredients

- ✓ 1 shallot, minced
- ✓ 1 cup Dry Riesling wine
- ✓ ½ cup honey
- ✓ 1 large bone-in smoked ham, about 10 lbs
- ✓ ¾ cup coarse grainy mustard

method

- ✓ For glaze, put the wine and shallots to a small saucepot and simmer. Reduce to ¼ cup. Lift pot from heat and stir in mustard and honey.
- ✓ Heat oven to 275F (135C). Put ham in a roasting pan and score the skin on top. Put in oven and bake for 7 hours. Do not cover it. Add half of glaze over ham and baste, cooking for 1 ½ hours more.
- ✓ Slice ham and serve with remaining glaze.

Roasted chicken with lemon and herbs

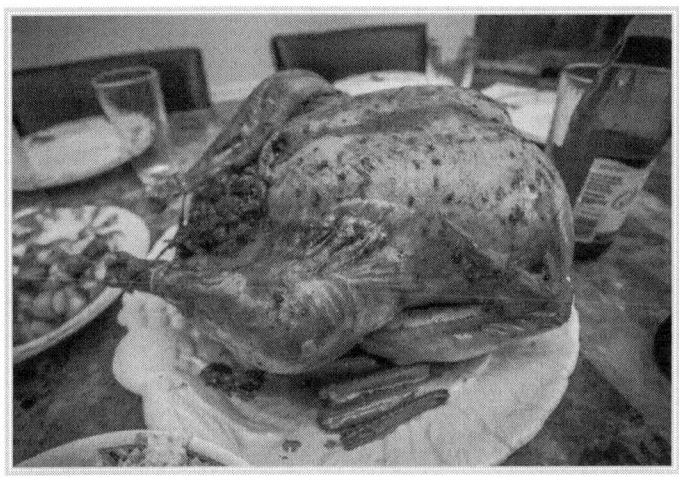

serves 4

ingredients

- ✓ 1 large chicken
- ✓ Several sprigs of fresh rosemary and thyme
- ✓ 1 lemon, cut into four slices
- ✓ 1 small onion, peeled and quartered
- ✓ 3 cloves garlic, whole
- ✓ 3 - 4 Tbsps olive oil
- ✓ Course ground pepper
- ✓ Sea salt

method

- ✓ Preheat oven to 400F (200C).
- ✓ Season and fill the chicken cavity with two of the lemon pieces, onion quarters, garlic, the whole herb sprigs, pepper, and salt. Truss the bird and spread the skin with olive oil, salt, and pepper and squeeze lemon juice on and around chicken.
- ✓ Put the chicken in a pan and roast for 1 hour, or until juices run clear.

Roast ham with stir fried veggies and mashed potatoes

SERVES 6

ingredients

- ✓ 5 large baking potatoes
- ✓ Water
- ✓ 1 Tbsp butter
- ✓ ¼ cup 1% milk
- ✓ 2 tsps prepared garlic (in a jar)
- ✓ ½ tsp pepper
- ✓ 1 tsp parsley flakes
- ✓ 1 can Ginger Ale (355 ml or12 oz)
- ✓ 1 cooked honey ham (4 lbs or 2kg)
- ✓ 4 cup fresh stir-fry mixed vegetables

- ✓ 1 tsp sesame oil
- ✓ 2 Tbsp teriyaki sauce
- ✓ Cooking spray
- ✓ Aluminum foil

method

- ✓ Boil water in a large stove-top pot.
- ✓ Cut potatoes in half, placing in a pot. Reduce heat to med-low when water comes to a boil.
- ✓ Cook the potatoes until ready for about 15 minutes
- ✓ Drain water from potato pot. Add milk, butter, garlic, pepper, and parsley to the potatoes.
- ✓ Mash together until smooth. (Try whipping potatoes with an electric beater).
- ✓ Let cool, then place in a microwave-safe pot or casserole with lid. Put in fridge.
- ✓ Preheat oven to 185F (85C). Sprays an oven-safe pan (same size as the ham) with cooking spray.
- ✓ Make tiny slits along the top of ham. Place ham in pan.
- ✓ Pour ginger ale over ham and cover tightly with foil or lid. Place in hot oven. Go off to work!!!
- ✓ Reset oven to 350F (175C). Remove foil from ham and leave ham in the oven.
- ✓ Place potatoes in the oven next to ham. Set timer for 20 minutes.
- ✓ Heat oil in a large wok at med-high heat.
- ✓ Add stir-fry mix to the pan and toss. Add teriyaki sauce.

- ✓ Toss vegetables until cooked through but lightly crisp.
- ✓ When the timer rings for ham, all is ready.

Roasted beet dip with goat cheese and hazelnuts

TIME 1 hour, 30 minutes

MAKES 2 1/2 cups

ingredients

- ✓ 1 Tbsp olive oil
- ✓ 1 1/2 pounds golden or red beets
- ✓ 5 sprigs thyme, divided
- ✓ 3/4 cup blanched hazelnuts (about 4 oz.)
- ✓ 1 large garlic clove, smashed
- ✓ 1/2 tsp kosher salt, divided
- ✓ 1/4 cup apple cider vinegar
- ✓ 1 Tbsp sugar
- ✓ 1/4 tsp whole black peppercorns
- ✓ 1 oz. (30g) goat cheese
- ✓ 1/4 tsp freshly ground black pepper
- ✓ Vegetable crudité and crackers (for serving)

method

- ✓ Heat the oven to 400F (200C). Clean beets and remove any spots. Set aside 1 small beet. Put a piece of aluminum foil on a rimmed baking sheet. Place remaining beets, oil, garlic, 3 thyme sprigs, and 1/4 tsp salt in the center of foil then wraps to close. Bake beets for 60–70 minutes until knife-tender. Let cool.
- ✓ Meantime, fry hazelnuts on another baking tray, occasionally tossing, for 6–8 minutes until golden brown.
- ✓ Cook 1/4 cup water, vinegar, peppercorns, sugar, and 1 thyme sprig, in a small pan over medium heat, mixing, until sugar is melted. Lift to a small bowl. Peel and thinly slice remaining beet into matchsticks and add to pickling liquid; liquid should cover all matchsticks. Let pickle while beets roast.
- ✓ When beets are chilled, carefully peel off skins. Pulse hazelnuts and 1/2 tsp thyme leave in a food processor until finely chopped. Add goat cheese, roasted beets, remaining 1/4 tsp salt, and 1/4 tsp ground black pepper, and pulse until smooth. Place in a serving bowl.

✓ Pulse 3 Tbsp pickled beets in a food processor until coarsely chopped. Mix into beet blend. Cover with remaining pickled beets and black pepper. Serve with crackers alongside and crudité.

Easy Christmas turkey

ingredients

- ✓ 4 lb (2kg) frozen rolled turkey breast
- ✓ 3 Tbsp olive oil
- ✓ 1 orange, juiced
- ✓ 0.4 oz (10g) butter
- ✓ 7 oz (200g) packet bought sage and onion stuffing
- ✓ 1 cup chicken stock
- ✓ 1 onion, chopped
- ✓ 4 Tbsp fresh herbs (e.g. flat-leaf parsley, rosemary, thyme)
- ✓ Gravy, to serve

method

- ✓ Heat oven to 350F (180C).
- ✓ Place turkey in the fridge and defrost turkey for 8-10 hours.
- ✓ Put the turkey in a large roasting pan with the foil on and roast for 1 h and 15 min.
- ✓ Remove from the oven and season with combined oil and orange juice.
- ✓ Leave foil off, return turkey to oven for another 30 min.
- ✓ For the stuffing, heat oil and butter in a frying pan over medium heat.
- ✓ Add the onion and cook until softened. Add the chicken stock and bring to the boil.
- ✓ Butter a lamington tray and spread stuffing into a tray, cover with aluminum foil and cook for 20 min (coincide with the last 30 min of cooking the turkey). Remove aluminum foil and cook for another 10 min.
- ✓ Transfer from heat. In a bowl, combine fresh herbs, stuffing mix, onion mixture, pepper and salt to taste.
- ✓ Cut the turkey, decorate with herbs and serve with warm gravy and stuffing.
- ✓ notes

✓ Cover the turkey with two layers of aluminum foil and it will keep warm while you prepare the beans and roast the potatoes.

✓ Use fresh herbs e.g. thyme, flat-leaf parsley, rosemary.

Open leftover Christmas ham sandwiches

ingredients

- ✓ 8 slices Christmas leg ham
- ✓ 8 slices soft cheese
- ✓ 4 thick slices bread
- ✓ ½ cup good quality egg mayonnaise
- ✓ 2 tsps. wholegrain mustard
- ✓ 2 ripe tomatoes, thickly sliced
- ✓ ½ cup small basil leaves

method

- ✓ Mix mayonnaise and mustard in a small bowl.
- ✓ For each sandwich, put 2 slices of ham on the toast, 2 slices of cheese top with some slices of tomato, and a sprinkling of basil leaves.

✓ Toast bread and spread with 1-2 Tbsp of mayo mixture.

Baked salmon

ingredients

- ✓ 1 side salmon (about 3 lbs or 1.5kg) skinned and pin boned
- ✓ 4 garlic cloves, crushed
- ✓ 2 lemons
- ✓ 1/3 cup extra-virgin olive oil and extra for drizzling
- ✓ 1 handful marjoram leaves
- ✓ 1 handful coriander leaves
- ✓ 1 handful flat-leaf parsley
- ✓ simple green salad or warm potato salad to serve

✓ **2 preserved lemon quarters**

method

- ✓ Heat oven to 350F (180C) or 320F (160C) fan-forced. Place salmon on a baking sheet.
- ✓ Finely grate the lemons' zest into a small bowl, add the oil and garlic and season to taste. Coat mixture all over the salmon. Slice the lemon into wedges and set aside for serving.
- ✓ Bake the salmon for 20-30 min or until just cooked.
- ✓ Meantime, soak the lemon quarters in cold water for 10 min. Remove the pulp and finely cut the zest. Combine the herbs with the preserved lemon zest and set aside.
- ✓ Put the salmon on a serving platter, drizzle with oil scatter over the herb mixture and serve with the salad and lemon wedges.

Sheet-pan chicken with sourdough and bacon

TIME:1 hr 5 mins

SERVES: 6

ingredients

- ✓ 1/2 pound (225g) piece bacon, cut into 1-by- 1/2-inch (1-2cm) pieces
- ✓ 1/2 pound (225g) sourdough boule, cut or torn into 2-inch pieces
- ✓ 1 large red onion, cut into 1-inch wedges
- ✓ 1 large baking potato—scrubbed, halved crosswise and cut into 3/4-inch wedges
- ✓ 2 Tbsp cold unsalted butter, diced
- ✓ 4 oregano sprigs

- ✓ 1/2 tsp crushed red pepper
- ✓ 1/4 cup extra-virgin olive oil
- ✓ Kosher salt
- ✓ Black pepper
- ✓ 6 whole chicken legs

method

- ✓ Heat the oven to 400F (200C). Toss the bacon, potato, bread, onion, butter, crushed red pepper, and oregano with the olive oil on a large rimmed baking tray and season generously with black pepper and salt. Spread in a flat layer. Season the chicken with black pepper and salt and arrange on the bread mixture.
- ✓ Roast the chicken and bread mixture for about 45 minutes, until the bread is crisp.
- ✓ Serve.

Holiday salad

TIME: 15 min

SERVES: 4

ingredients

- ✓ 2 lemons, juiced, plus 1/2 lemon
- ✓ 1/4 cup and 2 Tbsps extra-virgin olive oil
- ✓ 1 tsp sea salt
- ✓ 1/2 tsp freshly ground black pepper
- ✓ 5 medium heads Belgian endive, ends trimmed and cut into 1-inch rounds
- ✓ 1/4 pound (115g) Gruyere cheese, rind removed and diced into 1-inch (2.5cm) cubes

- ✓ 1 medium green apple, cored, peeled, and cut into 1-inch cubes
- ✓ 1/2 avocado, diced into 1-inch cubes
- ✓ 2 Tbsp dried cranberries or the seeds of 1 small pomegranate
- ✓ 2/3 cup defrosted corn kernels or 1/2 ear corn, cooked and kernels removed

method

- ✓ In a small pan mix the olive oil6 lemon juice, salt, and pepper. Set aside.
- ✓ Put the apples and endive into a large serving bowl. Press the juice of half a lemon into the bowl and spray to coat the apples and endive, so they don't turn brown. Add the avocado and cheese, and then add the cranberries and corn.
- ✓ Pour the dressing over the salad just before serving and toss to coat.

Kids – friendly Recipes

Cherry truffles

TIME 5 mins

SERVES: 70

ingredients

- ✓ 13 oz (375g) Nestlé sweetened condensed milk
- ✓ 13 oz (375g) Nestlé choc milk melts
- ✓ 7 oz (200g) Arnott's Choc Ripple biscuits, crushed
- ✓ 7 oz (200g) x 3 pkts Nestlé Plaistowe premium dark cooking chocolate, melted
- ✓ 1.8 oz (50g) Coles butter, chopped

- ✓ 3.5 oz (100g) Big Sister red glace cherries chopped
- ✓ Cadbury Bournville cocoa powder, for dusting

method

- ✓ Combine condensed milk and butter with melts in a medium heatproof pan. Place over a saucepan of boiling water over low temperature (make sure the pan doesn't reach the water). Mix for 4-5 minutes or until mixture is smooth and melted. Let cool.
- ✓ Add cherries and crushed biscuits. Stir to mix. Transfer to the fridge for about 1 hour until firm. Roll crowded tsps. of the mixture into balls and place in the fridge for 20 minutes.
- ✓ Dip all truffle into the melted chocolate then put on a tray lined with baking parchment to set. When chocolate is set, powder with cocoa powder to serve.

notes

- ✓ Dip the truffles in 2 or 3 batches of melted chocolate, as the chocolate will start to harden.

Or place the chocolate (in a heatproof pan) back over a saucepan of simmering water to melt if it is becoming to firm to dip. A stainless steel bowl or glass works well.

✓ Cold hands make rolling the truffles easier.

White chocolate and rice bubbles rocky road

TIME : 5 mins

SERVES: 20

ingredients

- ✓ 4.5 oz (125g) pink and white marshmallows, chopped coarsely
- ✓ 2 x 6 oz (180g) bar white eating chocolate, chopped coarsely
- ✓ 5 oz (150g) Turkish delight, chopped coarsely
- ✓ ¼ cup pistachios, chopped coarsely

- ✓ ¼ cup shredded coconut
- ✓ 2 Tbsps. shredded coconut, extra
- ✓ 1 cup Kellogg Rice Bubbles

method

- ✓ Grease 7.5in (19cm) deep square pan; line bottom and sides with 2 strips baking parchment, extending paper 0.8in (2cm) above sides.
- ✓ Mix chocolate with a metal spoon over medium heatproof bowl over the saucepan of boiling water until melted.
- ✓ Let cool 5 minutes.
- ✓ Mix remaining ingredients in large pan. Stir in chocolate, going quickly; spread mixture into pan.
- ✓ Strew over remaining coconut.
- ✓ Place in the fridge for 2 hours or until firm before slicing.

notes

- ✓ You can omit the Turkish delight and replace with more marshmallows.

✓ **You can use milk or dark chocolate instead of white chocolate.**

Rocky road

ingredients

- ✓ 3.5 oz (100g) marshmallows
- ✓ 1 lb (500g) dark chocolate
- ✓ 1 cup coconut
- ✓ 3.5 oz (100g) red glace cherries
- ✓ ½ cup peanuts
- ✓ ½ cup pistachios

method

- ✓ Melt chocolate in the microwave over medium heat. Cook for 2 min, stir, then cook another 2 minutes or until melted. Line a baking tray (6 x

10 x 1 in / 16 x 26 x 3 cm) with baking parchment, leaving 0.8 (2 cm) overhand each end.
- ✓ Cut cherries in half, cut marshmallows in half. Combine cherries, marshmallows, peanuts, coconut, and pistachios in a large bowl. Add melted chocolate and stir well to combine.
- ✓ Spoon into the baking tray and place in the fridge for at least 2 hrs. When set, transfer rocky road to a chopping board and cut into about 30 pieces.

notes

- ✓ This is an excellent idea for kids to make a gift for Dad. Use Dad's favorite nuts – cashews, hazelnuts, macadamias.

Christmas jellies

MAKES : 8 small glasses

ingredients

- ✓ 1 packet of passionfruit jelly
- ✓ 1 packet of lime jelly
- ✓ 1 packet of raspberry jelly
- ✓ Fresh berries or Christmas lollies to decorate

method

- ✓ Make red jelly and pour 1/4 cup into each cup, place in the fridge until set (4-6 hrs).

- ✓ Make yellow jelly, let it cool and add 1/4 cup carefully on red jelly. Return to fridge until set.
- ✓ Make green jelly, let it cool and add 1/4 cup carefully on yellow jelly. Return to fridge until set.
- ✓ Only before serving, decorate with berries or lollies.

notes

- ✓ Mix and match jelly colors as with Christmas or from your children's favorites.

Thank You for reading my book. I hope You enjoy these recipes.

With Christmas come Faith, Hope, and Love. I wish all these things for You and Your Family during the holiday season!

Sincerely, Nelly Grant

Manufactured by Amazon.ca
Bolton, ON

22223434R00042